POLICE OFFICERS

BY EMMA LESS

AMICUS READERS ● AMICUS INK

Amicus Readers and Amicus Ink are imprints of Amicus
P.O. Box 1329, Mankato, MN 56002
www.amicuspublishing.us

Cataloging-in-Publication Data is on file with the Library of Congress.
ISBN 978-1-68151-298-3 (library binding)
ISBN 978-1-68152-280-7 (paperback)
ISBN 978-1-68151-360-7 (eBook)

Editor: Valerie Bodden
Designer: Patty Kelley

Photo Credits:
Cover: Kali9/iStock
Inside: Alamy Stock: Mark Summerfield 6, Westend61 GmbH 10, Hunstock Images 12, Norma Jean Gargasz/Alamy Live 15,
Dreamstime.com: Frogtravel 16B, Shutterstock: A Katz 3, John Roman Images 5, Sintravelalat 8, David Sansegundo 16T,
Stephen Mulcahey 16R.

Printed in China.

HC 10 9 8 7 6 5 4 3 2 1
PB 10 9 8 7 6 5 4 3 2 1

Police officers watch us.
They keep us safe.

The officer
wears a badge.
She has a radio.

Police drive around towns. They make sure everyone follows the law.

They catch
people who steal.
They solve
crimes, too!

Oh no!
Jen's family
had a crash!
The police check
if anyone is hurt.

Sammy is lost.
The police help him
find his mom.

It's a parade.
Tim waves to
the officers.
He says thank you!

SEEN WITH THE POLICE

radio

patrol car

badge